Ready for School

Cassell Lifeguides

Cassell 'Lifeguides' are books for today's way of life. The increasing trend towards a 'self-help society' is an indication of the need for reliable, helpful information in book form, as less and less advice is offered elsewhere.

With this series, Cassell furthers its reputation as a publisher of useful, practical self-help books and tackles subjects which are very much in line with today's lifestyles and problems. As people become increasingly aware that situations need to be looked at from all sides, they can turn to these books for realistic advice and encouragement.

Setting up Home by Fiona Buchanan
Living with Teenagers by Tom Crabtree
Coping with Separation and Divorce by Jean Stuart
Staying Healthy by Mike and Tricia Whiteside
Ready for School by Maggie Wilson

Ready for School
Parents and teachers in partnership

Maggie Wilson

CASSELL

Cassell Publishers Limited
Artillery House, Artillery Row
London SW1P 1RT

© Maggie Wilson 1989

All rights reserved.
This book is protected by copyright.
No part of it may be reproduced,
stored in a retrieval system, or transmitted
in any form or by any means, electronic,
mechanical, photocopying or otherwise,
without written permission
from the publishers.

First published 1989

British Library Cataloguing in Publication Data
Wilson, Maggie
 Ready for school: parents and teachers in partnership.
 1. Pre-school children. Education by parents – Manuals
 I. Title
 372.13'02813

ISBN 0-304-32214-8

Typeset by Inforum Typesetting, Portsmouth
Printed and bound in Great Britain by Courier International Ltd,
Tiptree, Essex

Contents

1. Setting the scene 7
2. Ready for reading 10
3. Beginning to write 21
4. Fun with numbers 50
5. Kitchen science 60
6. Toys 70
7. Art and craft 74
8. Music at home 78
9. Body awareness 81
10. Getting on with others 84
11. Growing independence 87
12. Starting school 90
13. Summing up 92
    Book list 93
    Index 95

Acknowledgements

I would like to thank my husband, John, without whose support and encouragement the book would never have been written; my secretary, Margaret McDiarmid, and friend, Hazel Browning, who typed the manuscript; Florence Haward and Joyce Terrett, teachers; Chris Denton, Lyn Ryder, parents, who provided the examples of children's work; Barbara Lofthouse, Librarian, for help with the Book List; and the members of the Leicestershire Literary Support Team, from whom I have learned much during my years in Leicestershire.

1
Setting the scene

This book has been developed from talks I have given to local play group leaders, teachers and parents over many years. The demand for such talks does not diminish, and has led me to feel that what I have to say would be of interest to a wider audience.

I am the head teacher of a large village primary school, where I am responsible for 150 children aged from four to eleven plus. My own children have grown up, but even so it does not seem five minutes ago that I had three children under school age and was doing the shopping with one in the pram, one sitting on the pram seat and the third toddling along beside me. Perhaps this is a daily occurrence for you at the moment.

I don't know whether you are reading this as a parent, a play group leader, a teacher or a nursery nurse, but whoever you are I hope I can convince you of the importance, for learning, of the first five years of life for any child, and show you the ways in which you can make the best use of these early years.

Parents, play group leaders and others who have contact with pre-school children often express worries about what they should teach. I define education in terms of learning experiences, and learning how to learn, so parents and everyone working with young children can be just as much educators as school teachers can. This is one reason why I am always pleased to talk with parents, and would welcome the chance to talk with them on the day their child was born! Education begins at birth and what takes place during the pre-school years sets the foundation for future years.

I feel that I was lucky in being able to stay at home with my children until they had all reached school age. Later on, it was easy for me to resume full-time work, because I had the same hours and holidays as the children. Many mothers continue to work after the birth of their children, for a variety of reasons. Whatever decision you have made about work, I hope that the ideas in this book will help you in your children's pre-school years.

Parents have tremendous influence over their children in the early years. This is also true during the primary school years, because even when children are at school they still spend far more hours out of the school environment than within it. Consequently play groups and schools need the support of parents – 'Parents and Teachers in Partnership' would make a good motto for any play group or school.

If parents become worried about their child's schooling, they should approach the head teacher and express their fears. A school can do little unless it has the confidence of the parents. I always tell parents that the 'doors are open' and invite them to come in if they are worried about something, so that the 'molehill' doesn't grow into a 'mountain'. Even if you don't voice your worries at home the child will sense them, and then learning will be inhibited. Parents' worries can stem from the fact that schools today are very different from those they attended, and they 'don't do things the way they used to'. Parents may have had nothing to do with schools since they finished their own schooling, and moreover their memories may not be particularly happy ones! Much of my time is therefore spent in explaining to parents what is going on in the school and the educational thinking behind various activities. Once parents understand what is taking place and have confidence in the school, they relax. The children can then be educated in a happy, relaxed atmosphere.

My intention is that this book will help parents, and those who work with pre-school children, to prepare children for school in a way that will be enjoyable for all. When the children go to school the teacher can build on the firm foundations that have been laid during the first five years. The following chapters cover various aspects of learning and contain many practical suggestions, so that you can become actively involved in your children's learning. I have tried to give some indication of the ages at which children can be introduced to the various activities, but this is difficult because all children are individuals and will progress at different rates. This is perfectly natural, so please do not worry if another child appears to be learning at a much faster rate than your own. Comparisons can lead to unnecessary worry. Enjoy your children, and I hope that they will enjoy the activities mentioned in the following chapters.

2
Ready for reading

The majority of parents see reading as one of the most important skills that they want their child to learn. This activity certainly creates the most interest in the early years and questions about reading are often asked when parents and teachers meet. Most children learn to read at some point between the ages of four and a half and seven years but others can take much longer, and some may not become proficient readers until they are well into their teens. The foundations, however, can be laid during the pre-school years.

Speech begins to develop a few months after a baby has been born and continues to develop throughout the early years. The sounds that make up speech are learned at specific ages; this explains why children who have had a hearing problem may need speech therapy later to learn the sounds they have missed.

Many parents do not realize that language has to develop before reading can begin. A child has to internalize words before he or she can read them. Writing may well develop alongside reading, but spelling is usually fourth in the sequence. During my teaching career I have often found that a child who is slow to read was also slow to talk, and usually continues to have problems with writing and spelling until the reading ability increases.

TALKING TO THE BABY

Language is an area that parents can develop right from the cradle. This is why it is important to talk to babies when you are feeding, dressing or bathing them, and to chat to them when you are shopping or out for a walk. This does not mean a constant flow of conversation. You need a break and so does the baby. Everyone needs time to think, and silence can be 'golden'. Even so, comment on what you are doing and what you can see. It always worries me when parents tell me what a good baby their child was, and how he or she never cried and could be left for hours on end in the pram or cot. Babies should not be left alone for long stretches of time in the day. They need to be stimulated and talked to.

When children begin to speak they use single words. These words can be given several different meanings:

Dada – 'Hello Daddy' (when he comes back).
Dada – 'Come here, I want you.'
Dada – 'Please pick me up' (holding out hands).

You can probably think of many more examples, depending upon the circumstances in which the word is used. The same can be said of the word 'no', which is quickly learned!

Soon the children learn to string two or three words together, although they do not necessarily put them together in the order you would use. For example:

'Mama dog look' probably means
'Look at the dog'.

You can extend your children's language by adding to what they have said:

'Mama dog ball' could become
'Yes, look at the dog playing with the ball'.

Later this can be extended even further:

'Yes, look at the big brown dog playing with the red ball'.

You will find that children learn by example. Gradually their simple sentences will become more complex. They also generalize. For instance, they may know the words cooked, looked, painted, and so may well use runned, maked, swimmed or eated. Use the correct form in your answer. This is better than obviously correcting and so turning your conversation into a grammar lesson! They may also generalize in other ways. For example, every four-legged animal may be called a dog, or every four-wheeled vehicle a car. This is quite usual, but it isn't long before the child can differentiate between such words.

Gradually you can extend children's language even further by asking them to tell you what might be going to happen and why, or perhaps to imagine what it would be like to do something or to go somewhere. You could, for instance, talk about dreams, fears, flying or visiting a strange place. You can probably think of a much longer list, but this will give you an idea.

By this time you also need a bottomless pit of patience to help you deal with questions such as 'why, how, when?' 'Because I say so' may give you some peace, but it is not a great help in language development! If you try to cope with all these queries you will provide a valuable learning experience for the child.

SHARING BOOKS

I talk of sharing books with children because 'sharing' creates a different atmosphere from reading books 'to' children or, later, insisting that children read books 'to' you. The idea of sharing makes for a more relaxed situation. Sit in a comfortable chair, with the child either on your lap or snuggled up beside you. The physical contact is vital.

I don't think of books as children's books or adult books, and I agree with C.S. Lewis, who divided books into good and bad ones. In other words, if a book is well written and has something to say, an adult will enjoy it just as much as a child. Even if you have many books at home that you share with the children, don't forget to explore and exploit your local library to the full. Most libraries nowadays have a children's librarian. Get to know him or her and find out when there will be story sessions and other activities in the library. Let the children help with the selection of books. They should have their own library card as soon as possible.

When looking at books together do not forget to talk about the parts of a book: the cover, the spine, the title, the author, the

Ready for reading

illustrator, the pages. Show the children how to turn pages correctly and remind them to have clean hands before looking at a book. Afterwards remind them to replace the book on the shelf. If they learn that books are precious possessions they will always value reading.

I want to make a plea for books without text. I feel sure that you will happily use cloth and board books with your two- and three-year-olds, but once they enjoy a story you may easily overlook books without text. Yet picture books are marvellous for getting children to talk about what they think will happen next. This can be called extending prediction skills, and is very good for stretching the imagination. You can talk about the picture on the page, then ask the child what will happen next. Perhaps the child had the same idea as the author, perhaps a different one. Either way it does not matter, as long as the child can justify the choice.

Many books for young children repeat words or phrases and this helps them learn to read, because the repetition of printed symbols helps the child connect the spoken words with the symbols on the page. Children often have a favourite story. You have to read this every night, and woe betide you if you leave anything out! The favourite with my children was 'Jack and the Beanstalk'. Even if you are going out, and you are late, you must read every word! The children learn it off by heart, and then you will find them sitting 'reading' – pointing to the words and turning over pages, albeit in odd places. The important thing is that they think they are reading. Please don't squash them by telling them that they have only memorized the words, because memory training is a vital step in learning to read. The next section will give you some ideas on this.

MEMORY GAMES

You can develop memory by teaching jingles and finger-play rhymes, nursery rhymes and songs. I am sure that you sing the traditional nursery rhymes at home, or to pass the time on a journey. Then after the bath when you are drying hands or feet you can say:

This little piggy went to market.
This little piggy stayed at home.
This little piggy had roast beef.
This little piggy had none.
And this little piggy cried wee, wee, wee,
All the way home.

When the children go to play school (if you are lucky enough to have one near you) they will learn many other finger-play rhymes, such as:

Tommy Thumb, Tommy Thumb.
Where are you? Where are you?
Here I am, here I am.
How do you do, how do you do, etc.

This is said, starting with all the fingers hidden in the palm of the hand, and bringing each one out as it is called for. This can prove quite difficult for adults as well as children. If you have not done it before, see how you get on when Ruby Ring is called, that is the third or ring finger! If you would like to learn more of these rhymes you will find the book list on page 93 useful.

You could also play games such as Kim's Game, in which you place various items on a tray on the floor, let the child look at them for a minute, then cover them and see how many are remembered. Another game is I Went Shopping, in which each person in turn says 'I went shopping and I bought . . .', and with each turn the shopping list lengthens. The items bought could tie in with a specific letter sound. For example, for A: 'I went shopping and I bought six apples, an antelope, four axes, an alligator', and so on, until someone forgets an item. Memory, however, is only one of the activities connected with learning to read. There is more about others in the following sections.

LISTENING

Do your children listen intently to what you say, to tapes, to the radio or to the television? Many teachers feel that children do not listen as well as they might and perhaps you feel the same. When your children watch television, watch the programmes with them so that afterwards you can discuss what you have seen. However, don't let the television become a child minder! Television can certainly take us to far-away places, is instructive and can extend vocabulary. Even so it does not always stretch the imagination as much as listening to the radio or a tape, because television is first and foremost a visual stimulus. Play story cassettes and records for the children to listen to, and listen to the radio with them so that they can learn to listen without the help of anything visual. Again, if you can listen together so much the better. Since BBC radio has little to offer young children except 'Listening Corner', which is only a five-minute programme, you could try some of the schools' programmes, such as 'Poetry Corner'.

MUSIC AND RHYTHM

Music and rhythm are also important in learning to read. Words have a rhythm of their own, and enjoyment of music and its rhythms helps early reading. Dr Audrey Wisbey, in her book *Learn to Sing to Learn to Read*, takes this point even further.

Music in one form or another is available to all children, for example 'Top of the Pops', the various BBC wavelengths and local radio; then there are tapes and records, and these can be borrowed from your local library. Some children will be lucky enough to have parents or older brothers and sisters who play instruments, while others will be able to enjoy listening to the piano being played at play group. Don't forget that you can make instruments at home, and enjoy making music there with a variety of shakers, water in jars, sticks or cutlery banged on a tin, even tissue paper on combs. You can make various shakers from tins and plastic containers filled with varying amounts of rice, lentils, split peas, seeds, beads, bottle tops, coins or pegs. Try anything that is to hand until you achieve a sound that the children like.

Children should also be encouraged to walk and move in a variety of ways in time with the music; they can clap out rhythms and sing. Singing nursery rhymes can be fun for everyone. Can the

16 Ready for School

children recognize them if you just clap out the rhythm? Can they recognize their own name when the rhythm is clapped? There is music in every child, it just needs to be brought out. Chapter 8 will take these points further.

RECOGNIZING SHAPES

Shape is another area of pre-reading activity. I expect that you have at home jigsaw puzzles of varying difficulty. If you have a child who can do them easily, try turning them upside down so that they can only be done by shape rather than with the picture to help. I don't know your feelings about comics, but they can be very useful in the teaching of reading. Comics often contain a puzzle page, and two favourite items are finding the differences between two very similar pictures and finding 'hidden' items in a picture. Both these activities help the development of shape discrimination. Later, when the children are beginning to learn to read, they will often learn individual words by recognizing their shapes:

|aeroplane| and |elephant|

These words have two very different outlines – there is more about this in the next chapter.

FOLLOWING A SEQUENCE

The ability to sequence also needs to be developed during the early years, and many activities can aid this. Sequencing just means sorting items into a specific order. Many things in everyday life have to be correctly ordered or sequenced, or the results will be very haphazard. When you are cooking you have to add the ingredients in the correct order or the end product may be uneatable. When you are dressing you need to put your clothes on in a certain sequence or you may look rather bizarre! Reading also depends upon certain sequences. In Britain most of us read books from the front to the back, and on each page we read from left to right starting at the top left-hand side. Sequencing activities should therefore bear this in mind.

Here are some ideas for you to try out.

1. Colour a repeating sequence:

● ● ○ ● ● ○ ● ● ○ ● ● ○
red　blue　yellow　r　b　y　r　b　y　r　b　y

2. Thread beads in a given order:

3. Thread beads according to size, shape and colour:

r　b　r　g　y　g

4. Draw an easy sequence:

ı|　ı|　ı|　ı|　ı|

5. Draw harder sequences:

|o□|　|o□|

6. Ask children to walk in a certain sequence:
two steps then a jump, two steps then a jump,
walk four, run four, etc.

7. Ask them to repeat a series of claps:
three even claps

Gradually give harder patterns to echo:
two slow, two quick, one slow

8. Sing something for them to repeat:
the start of a song,
up or down the scale.

9. Again comics can be useful, and when they are old they can be cut up. A story can be cut up into its separate frames, and then the child can be asked to sort them out to tell a story. Don't worry if they are not put into the order you expected. Any order is perfectly acceptable as long as the sequence can be justified. Remember that the story should 'read' from left to right.

UNDERSTANDING BOOKS

Reading should always go hand-in-hand with understanding. You don't want your children to experience reading simply as the ability to break a code, nor do you want them to 'bark at print' in a senseless way. Consequently, even at the very earliest stages you need to check that the children are understanding what is being read to them and, later, that they understand what they are reading as they read it. As adults, and particularly as teachers and parents, we sometimes assume too much. Talk about the book being read, ask questions about what has happened and what might happen next. Encourage children to use their imagination so that they can get 'under the skin' of the characters within the book, and the various events that take place.

Don't be tempted to buy reading schemes for your children. There *are* some good ones, but at the same time there are some appalling ones. Using schemes can lead to unhelpful competition and to the idea that children read reading scheme books until they can read, then are allowed to read 'real' books. You can avoid these problems by using 'real' books right from the start. You will find suggestions in the Book List on page 93 and your local children's librarian will be ready to help you, too.

CONCLUSION

This outline of pre-reading stages and skills is very brief because this book is not a textbook on reading. However, if I now list the stages in the use of books during the pre-school years it will be helpful.

1. Cloth, waterproof and board books. These can be looked at in the bath, in bed, when you are sitting together and on a journey. These books will probably have only one object in each picture, and they will be clear and in bold colours. Talk about the pictures, and let the child help you to turn the pages. Gradaully the child will learn how to hold a book and turn the pages in succession without your help.

2. Picture books with more detail. Talk about the pictures, what is happening in them, what the people are like, what they might do next, etc.

3. Picture books with captions. Talk about the pictures first, and what you both think is going to happen. Then go back to the start and read the captions pointing to the words as you say them. If the book has a recurring phrase or refrain, encourage the child to join in each time the phrase is repeated. Afterwards, see if the child can retell the story in his or her own words.

4. Picture books with more detail and description. Use these as in stage 3. In this way you will stretch the child's imagination as well as making sure that meaning goes hand-in-hand with reading from the beginning stages.

5. Picture books with more text to read. Again use these as above.

6. Taped stories to go with a picture book. These tapes often use a buzzer or other device to tell when to turn the page.

7. By this time your child may be reading, or at least memorizing a favourite book.

8. Some children do learn to read before they go to school, but most learn while they are in the infant part of the primary school. Either way, if you have shared books with your child, and continue to do so, you have laid the foundations for reading.

Last, but by no means least, before I leave this 'thumb-nail sketch' of pre-reading, I will once more mention enjoyment. This is in many ways the key to the whole activity, and indeed to any activity you may undertake at home. You can't go far wrong if you make the experience a happy one, and one to be looked forward to, rather than dreaded. In the previous chapter I mentioned that a happy relaxed atmosphere creates the ideal setting for learning, and throughout the rest of the book I will continue to emphasize this point. Perhaps it is the 'bee in my bonnet', but you can decide that for yourself!

3
Beginning to write

NOT ALL IN CAPITALS!

Children of four, and sometimes even younger, usually want to learn to write. If they are keen they should be helped from the start to form letters correctly, rather than allowed to form bad habits that can be difficult to eradicate. Teaching children to write using only capital letters creates an enormous problem for teachers because this habit is hard to break. When a child shows a teacher a picture and proudly points to where she or he has signed her or his name, the teacher is torn between saying, 'Well done, you are clever writing your own name on your painting', and thinking, 'Oh dear, another child who only knows how to write capital letters.' I know that we need to use capital letters when filling in forms, and at the start of sentences and names, but we use small, or lower-case, letters more often. It is the lower-case letters that give words their shape, and these shapes are important in learning to read (as I mentioned in the previous chapter). This point will be expanded further in the section called 'Writing my name' on page 25.

SCRIBBLE

The earliest stage of writing is when children hold a thick crayon or pencil, wrapping their whole hand around it, and happily scribble away on a large piece of paper. Children as young as two may do this, although most will be three before they really gain pleasure from making marks on paper. This is a form of exploratory play, and children gain much satisfaction from the gradual improvement

22 Ready for School

in their control of a crayon or pencil. By the time they are four their 'scribbles' become more representational and the children will tell you what they have drawn even if you have difficulty in deciding what it might be. The example of Penelope's snake illustrates this. She knew it was a snake even if her mother wasn't so sure!

The scribble stage therefore leads on to creative art as well as to writing. Encourage your child to draw and paint and to develop artistically. I will say more about this in Chapter 6, but for the moment just be careful that you don't push writing before your child is really ready.

A doggie

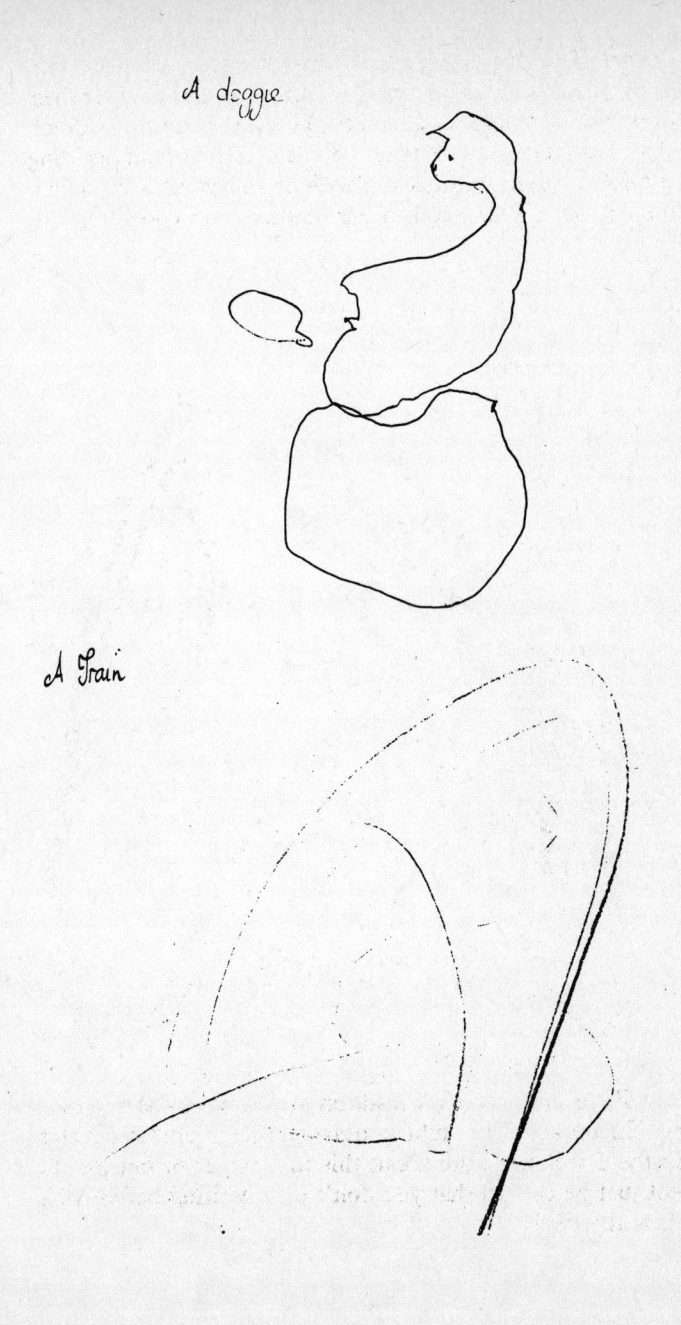

A Train

A Pony.

BEGINNING TO WRITE

When your child does want to write he or she will make it plain, because they will state their wish very clearly. Children of four years usually want their marks to look more like 'real' writing, and their name is frequently the word with which they want to start.

Writing should be done not just for its own value but for a reason. So once children can write their names they can write at the end of letters, on cards, on paintings and even on notes to the milkman or shopping lists. Don't worry if your child holds the pencil in one hand one day, and the other the next. This is quite natural. Gradually a preference will be shown for either the left or right hand. If your child prefers to use the left hand, make sure the paper is well to the left of him or her so that the writing can be unrestricted. This will prevent turning of the paper or an odd grip of the pencil. The children should also be encouraged to write from left to right.

WRITING MY NAME

When your child wants to learn to write his or her name, use plain paper and don't write the name all in capitals, just the initial as a capital letter with the rest of the word in lower-case letters. This is not only the correct way of writing any name, it also means that the child begins to learn to recognize the shape of the word. You will remember that shape discrimination plays an important part in learning to read. If you write names in capital letters the shapes formed are always rectangles, albeit of varying size:

| ANN | ANDREW | MARY | PATRICIA |

On the other hand, if you write only an initial capital, the shapes formed are much more distinctive, and therefore more easily memorized:

Ann Andrew Mary Patricia

CONFUSING SMALL WORDS

The individual shape of a word helps a child to recognize its own name. This is also why children can quickly learn to read long words like elephant or aeroplane, but have problems with smaller works such as saw/was or on/no.

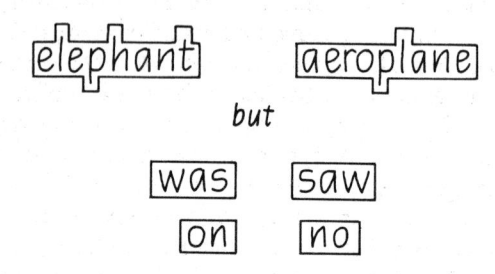

elephant   aeroplane

but

was   saw
on   no

Words with the same letters, but in different orders, are difficult for children to read for another reason too. When a child plays with a doll or a train, it stays a doll or a train whether it is upside down or the right way up. Unfortunately, letters and words are not so kind to us, and can change into something completely different as soon as their position is altered:

$$b \rightarrow d \qquad m \rightarrow w$$
$$n \rightarrow u \qquad p \rightarrow q$$

was → saw   on → no   now → won
from → form   left → felt

LETTER FORMATION

If your child wants to learn to write, I would suggest that you ask your local school which handwriting scheme they use, because there are quite a variety. Here is the one used in my school.

Beginning to write 27

a b c d e f g h i j k l m
n o p q r s t u v w x y z

When I taught reception children, I began with the children's names, and whenever the children did some 'writing' or a painting I asked them to sign their name underneath like an author or an artist. I would then take families of letters to practise their correct formation, and gradually extended to the whole alphabet. Stick letters, such as l, t, k, i, b, p, are the easiest ones; then go on to rounded letters, o, c, a, d, g, q, etc. It is important that children learn to start the letters in the correct place, and finish in the correct place, so that later on they won't have problems in joining their letters together. Pencil grips can help children who find it difficult to hold a pencil correctly. These can be made at home, by cutting a hole in some sponge rubber and placing this over the pencil, or they can be bought commercially. Traffic lights, that is, green dot as starting point and red dot as finishing point, and arrows showing direction, can help correct formation.

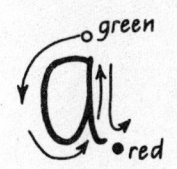

Encourage the children to make the letters large, on large plain sheets of paper. They will also enjoy writing them in wet sand, with a wet finger on a formica top, or with paint on paper – but not, I hope, on the wallpaper or paintwork! It helps the children to memorize various letter shapes if you turn writing into a physical activity and form the letters by drawing them in the air as large as possible, stretching up as high as you can, out as far as you can and right down to the floor. Descriptions can also help remind children about formation:

b, a bat then a ball

d, the dog comes through the door followed by its tail

Many children confuse b and d, and confusion can often continue until they are seven years old, so don't worry if your children have a problem in the pre-school years. Some children find it helpful to make those letters with their hands and think of the word 'bed'.

left hand – b					right hand – d

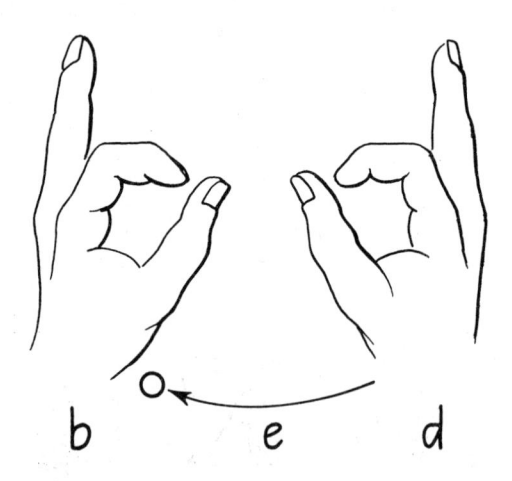

Some children of junior school age still find this a useful *aide-mémoire*, even though they do it under the table or desk!

o = green   • = red

LETTER NAMES OR SOUNDS?

Mention of handwriting and letter formation usually brings with it the question, 'Do I teach the letter names or sounds?' I feel it is important that children realize that a letter has a name, as well as one or more sounds, and also that a letter has two shapes, upper-case and lower-case. This helps to avoid confusion later. If a child has been taught the sounds at home, it can be very difficult to accept letter names, or that c̄ can suddenly become č, or ḡ become ǧ as in

c̄at, čeiling ḡarage, ǧiraffe

Alphabet books can be useful, but on the whole they only show one picture for each letter, so children can tend to connect only one object with each letter. Why not make your own book at home, and for each letter show the capital and lower-case form, as well as a variety of items for each letter? The children will enjoy helping you, and will like a drawing or photo of themselves on their letter's page.

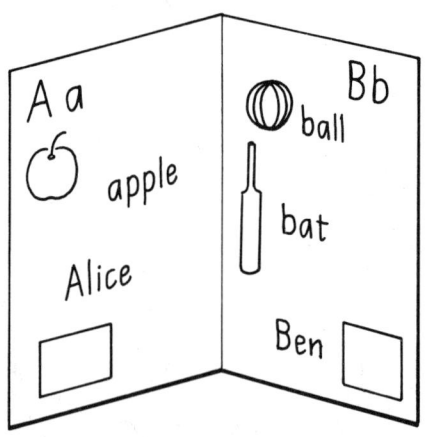

A pictogram is a letter turned into a character or object. Lyn Wendon's pictogram alphabet is a delightful way of learning not only the alphabet, but also letter formation – capitals and lower-

Beginning to write 31

case. She has worked out stories and characters to explain why the letters are the shapes they are. Great fun to use! You will find this on the Book List.

FROM SCRIBBLE TO CREATIVE WRITING

Once a child becomes interested in writing and learning about letters, you need to understand that there are many stages to be gone through between scribbling and becoming an independent writer. Most children manage these stages somewhere between the ages of two and seven. Consequently, most of the stages will take place after your child starts school. Pre-school children may manage stages 1–3, while stages 4–7 will take place in the infant classes. I have included stage 8 on spelling for general interest, although most of this work will take place in junior classes. You will find it of use later on, or now if you have children aged between seven and eleven. Here are some examples of the stages.

1. Scribble. The child will know what has been 'written' even if you are unsure!

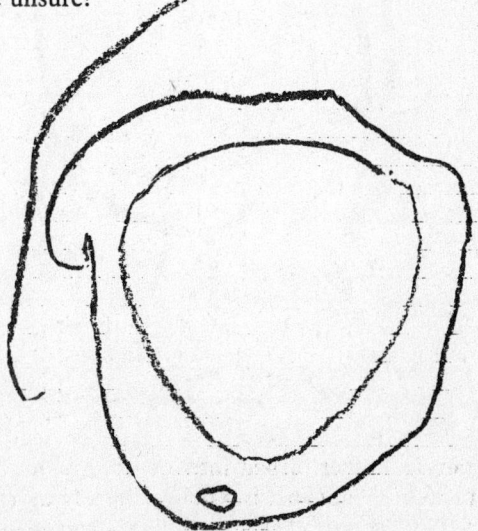

Snowman and 'Christmas man' with writing. The words on the drawings opposite were written by adults.

My daddy sits

and reads

his paper.

the water

Mr Noah and his ark

34 Ready for School

2. The child writes over your writing – from now on *always* watch for correct formation – use traffic lights or anything to help this, and correct direction, i.e. left to right.

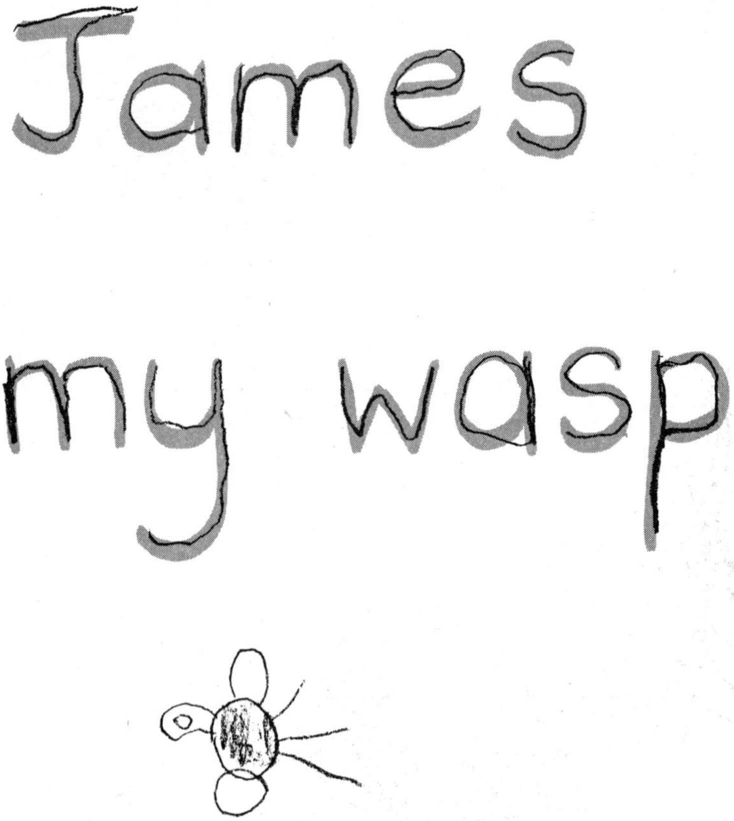

James

my wasp

Oliver

my spiders

36   Ready for School

N.B. If this is very difficult, draw wide 'roads' for the child to draw lines inside, then gradually decrease the width of 'road'.

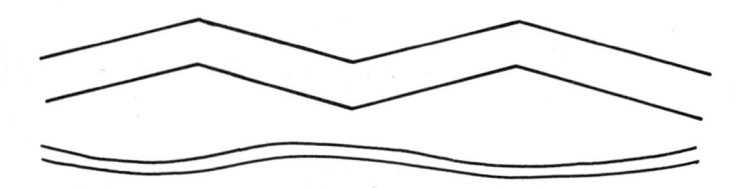

Then try going over your writing once more.

3. Dot the letters, and the child joins them up. Start with closely placed dots, and gradually space them out.

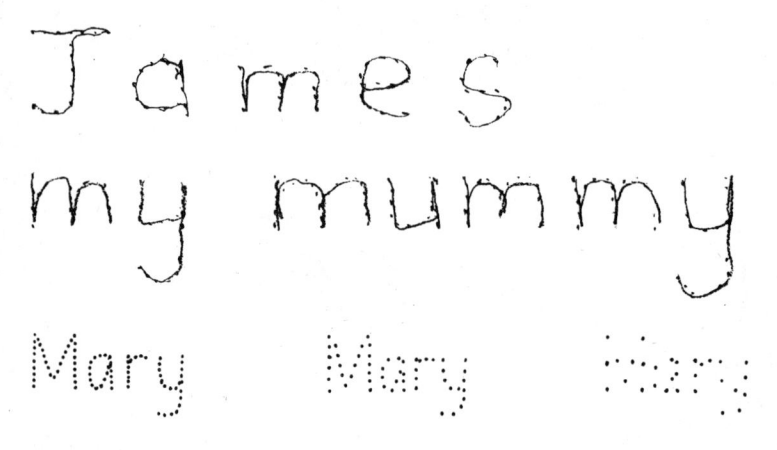

James

my mummy

Mary   Mary   Mary

4. You write what the child wants to say. Then the child copies underneath.

Kate   my   house

Katₑ   my   house

Christopher

Christopher

Christopher

We decorated our
we decorated our

christmas tree
christmas tree

James
catherine

We decorated our
we decorated our

christmas tree
christmas tree

Merry Christmas
Merry Chistmas

Love from Alice.
Lov from Alice.

Beginning to write 39

5. You write on a piece of paper what the child wants to say. The child copies this on to another piece of paper. N.B. This is a very difficult stage and children need much practice at this level – their handwriting often deteriorates for a time.

James

Chrismas tree

we Decorate our

we decorated our

christmas tree

Merr chrismas

Love from Alice

40 Ready for School

6. The child begins to write a few words unaided, but asks you for the others. Ask the child to tell you the beginning letter of the word, and as many others as possible. Spelling is now beginning.

7. Gradually the child is able to write more words unaided, but will need a personal dictionary for you to write the unknown words in. This will build up into a word bank for future use. Any small notebook will do, and if you give each letter a page the child will be learning alphabetic order at the same time. Mark each page with the capital and lower-case forms: Aa, Bb, etc.

> The windy day
>
> one day I went to the shops and wind started to blow the door slamed and the notice on the door turned over and I thoght that the shops was closed so I went home and flew my kite and the door slamed and I could not open the door and mummy was the nextdoor neighbour we had to sleep at nanas and still could not get in so we waited for daddy when daddy come back from woke we we home I went to bed and in the morning my skirt blew off the washing line so the months passed with the windy days and they were hap one day the wind blew a tree down I bet they were glad when summer came.

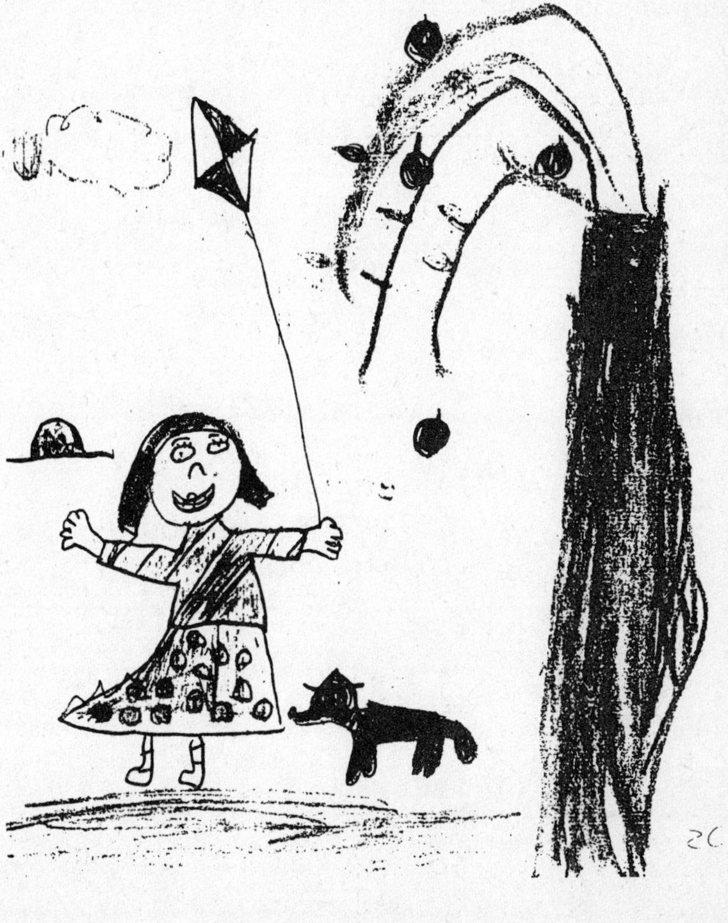

The windy Day

One day I was going for a walk and the wind began to blow it blew my hat off and it blew my hair and then a treee fell dawn I ran home and told mumm and she said lets have a look so we went to the place where I had seen it and mummy said we can't lift it ourselves I will go and ask our next door neighbour to come and help us you come with me so I went and we went to see if our neighbour woud help us but she was out so we left it and went home and had a cup of tea and went to bed till morning.

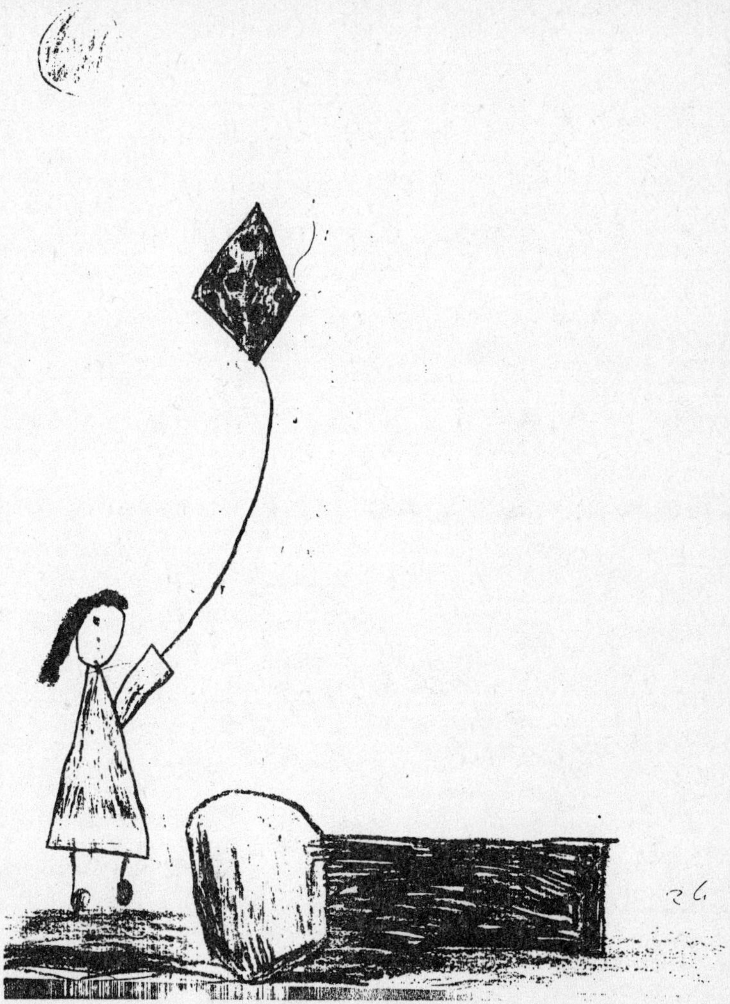

a windy Day

one day when I was playing in the garden and my Mummy was putting her washing up when suddenly her washing line snapped. I went inside to tell Daddy.

said that he
would ring his friend
Red they fixed
the washing line.
again for Mummy
Mummy had to wash
the washing again.

The windy day

One day I whent to my next door neighbour and the wind was blaiing and I heard my door slam and my mummy was out of my house but my next door neighbour had another key so that my mummy and me could get in and then my Daddy came home and then we had tea and then I whent

to bed but I could not
get to sleep because
the wind was blowing ✓

Went

Well done

a windy day

one day I was outside and the washing was on the line and the door slamed and one of my skirts fell off the washingline and it went oevr a tree in aur back garden and I went to go in But I could not get in I did not hafe a key and I did not hafe a coat on And I only had my slippers on I felt cold I coud feel the wind on me and I was along there was noone else out side noone efen saw me not even my mummy of my daddy saw me I was Frightened I went in to a bush and to kepp my feet warm and my Hands warm and all my body instead of getting it cold but I still shivered a bit and I shivered a bit more and then the door flew open and my mummy came out and my dog jumped out at me and then my other dog jumped out at me I was pleased that my mummy had found me ✓

Well done
Laura
26

8. As the child learns to write more words, write the unknown words on a piece of paper, but don't let the child take it to where she or he is writing. Encourage the child to look at the word and try to memorize it, then go back to write it unaided. Children

only learn to spell if they learn to put effort into it. Most of us also need a strategy for learning to spell words:

mispronouncing – *Wed nes* day.

saying – Th . . sday, what's missing?
You are, Thursday.

rhythm – bi-cy-cle, bicycle.
(This can help with learning the alphabet too.)

mnemonics – because, <u>b</u>ig elephants <u>c</u>atch <u>a</u>nts <u>u</u>nder <u>s</u>mall <u>e</u>lephants.

seeing connections between words – <u>do</u>, <u>do</u>es, <u>do</u>n't, <u>do</u>ne.
(They all contain <u>do</u> even if they are pronounced differently.)

Perhaps your child will need to use a variety of strategies; it doesn't matter how many, as long as they work. Some people are lucky, they seem to be natural spellers. Most of us, however, have to work at it!

I have gone into some detail in setting out these stages in learning to write, because you may find it interesting to know just how many stages there are. However, please don't see these stages as a 'home curriculum'. Most of the stages will take place after the children start school.

Earlier in the book I mentioned that children need to work at their own pace and this applies to handwriting. So you may well find that the ages I have attached to the stages do not apply to your child. Nor have I mentioned correcting your child's writing, because in many ways this does not apply. I would suggest that you correct the formation of letters if you see them being formed incorrectly, and that you encourage your child to spell his or her name correctly. Once more remember not to push an activity, and don't force your children to do something if they are not interested or not ready to tackle it. The key word is still enjoyment!

4
Fun with numbers

Learning letter formation leads on to interest in number symbols. Numbers play an integral part in everyday life and mathematics stems from these daily activities. Everyone uses mathematics to solve a variety of problems each and every day, and this is what I call 'real' maths. Yes, children in school are asked to do sums in books, but this is for practice and is only a small part of their mathematical development. Pre-school children have many mathematical experiences every day, but these should be of a practical nature and not recorded. Later, when they are at school, the work will initially be verbal and only gradually will recorded work be introduced. Here are some useful mathematical experiences that can be started as soon as children are interested.

SORTING

Young children need to experience a wide variety of sorting activities, such as these:

1. They can help you sort out the clothes ready for the washing machine into whites, coloureds and woollens.
2. When you do the ironing they could put the finished items into piles ready for the airing cupboard.
3. A button box can give endless hours of enjoyment. The children will enjoy feeling the various buttons as well as sorting them in a variety of ways: by size, by colour, those with two holes, those with four holes, etc.

Fun with numbers 51

4. They can sort the cutlery after the washing-up, and put it back in the cutlery drawer.
5. Shells collected on holiday can give plenty of sorting practice.

These are just a few ideas for you to try out, and I'm sure you can think of many more.

Sorting can be done according to a variety of attributes: colour, size, weight, shape, materials used in manufacture, etc. Gradually children can be encouraged to sort according to two or more attributes, but many children will probably be five years or older before managing this activity.

I tried one idea out with my own children when we were spring-cleaning the kitchen and all the various spoons were lying on the table. We started by sorting them into those that needed polishing and those that didn't, and after that it became a game to see how many different ways we could sort them:

to be polished	not to be polished
made of metal	not made of metal
made of plastic	not made of plastic
with wooden handles	without wooden handles
with holes	without holes
those we could see through	those we couldn't see through

(they enjoyed learning the words opaque and transparent)

used for cooking	used for eating

big ones   medium-sized ones   small ones

The kitchen didn't get cleaned very quickly but we all had fun with the sorting. An activity such as this not only creates fun, but also stimulates discussion and extends vocabulary.

COUNTING

Pre-school children need experience of counting. By this I mean becoming aware of the 'oneness of one', not just being able to recite a string of numbers, or a number rhyme such as:

> One two three four five,
> Once I caught a fish alive.
> Six seven eight nine ten,
> Then I let him go again.
> Why did you let him go?
> Because he bit my finger so.
> Which finger did he bite?
> This little finger on the right.

I'm sure you will have seen children happily saying 'one, two, three', etc., while counting beads or bricks, but not saying a number for each item counted. The answer given does not usually tie up with the number of items counted. This means that the child does not yet know the 'oneness of one' and is not in fact counting.

Your house and the local environment give endless possibilities for counting:

Fun with numbers

1. You can count the stairs, and later count them going up in twos.
2. When setting the table count how much cutlery is needed altogether, as well as how many individual knives, forks, spoons, plates and glasses are required.
3. Ask how many biscuits or sweets are in the tin, and when you have had one each ask how many are left in the tin.
4. You can use anything at hand for counting practice, but if you want to turn counting into a daily game you could put specific items in a set place each day and ask your child to count them. Vary the amount each day, starting with numbers up to five, and only when these numbers can be counted accurately extended to ten.
5. It is a good idea for you to encourage 'estimation' from the beginning by asking, 'How many things do you think there are?' The initial answer will be wild guesses, but gradually the estimates will become more accurate. Estimation is an important part of mathematics.
6. It is interesting to see what happens when you space out the objects to be counted, or put them close together, or place them in a disorganized fashion.
7. Begin with objects that the children can touch, and say a number as they feel each item. Later, progress to objects that can only be pointed at rather than touched. After this it is a good idea to move on to items that have to be waited for, cars or lorries, for example. Add on one at a time, and remember to ask, 'How many now?' It is encouraging when the children can say the next number without recounting from the beginning each time.

Counting can also be connected with pattern making and sequencing. The activities in Chapter 2 in the section on 'Following a sequence' (p. 17) illustrate this. You could extend activities 1, 2 and 3 further by asking for varying amounts of each colour or shape. For example, in activity 1, colour three red, two blue and one yellow, or any other variation you can think of, although I would suggest that you make five the highest amount. In activity 6, sequencing and counting can become a dance-like activity.

MEASURING

Length

Measuring should be done using a variety of units, such as hands, feet, cotton reels, straws or anything else that is handy to use. Children at school measure in this way, too, and only when they are seven or older do they begin to use the metric system. By all means use the metric measurements when you talk to the children, but let them use objects in their measurements. At first it is easier to use plentiful items so that they can be placed along the object being measured and remain there to be counted. Later the children can count as they use their hands or feet, but quite often they will need to measure several times because they will forget the number they have reached. If this leads to frustration they can cut out several paper hands or feet and use these in the same way as cotton reels. The children will be interested to know their height, and a wall chart on their bedroom door showing their height and date of measurement will be of interest to you, too. Once more remember that estimation should always be encouraged in mathematical activity.

Weighing

The children's own weight will be a source of interest to you all, and although body weight will be given in kilograms, other weighing should be done using arbitrary measurements rather than standard ones. Cooking, of course, gives marvellous opportunities for weighing and the children will enjoy helping you, especially if they can taste the end product. This will, however, also use standard weights. When the children weigh on their own I would suggest that they use a two-pan balance. These are not expensive and can be obtained from most toy shops, or the education departments of larger stores. The children can then enjoy using a variety of items to balance the scales:

> How many marbles will balance a wooden brick?
> How many pegs will balance a small ball?
> How many wooden bricks will balance a book?

There are endless opportunities for weighing activities of this kind. If you have the time, make up parcels so that the children can discover that large items do not necessarily weigh more than small ones. Young children tend to believe that the larger the object is, the heavier it will be. Don't forget to encourage the children to estimate before they weigh objects.

Capacity

This is the measurement of how much a container can hold e.g. how much water or sand. These activities connect up well with water play, which will be mentioned again later in the book. The children will hear you speak of pints of milk but in school children use metric measurements. Once again, however, young children and infant children should use a variety of objects for arbitrary measuring, such as cups, spoons, beakers, bottles, jugs, tins and so on. They can have great fun seeing how many cupsful will fill a bucket, how many jugsful will fill the washing-up bowl, etc. Bathtime can be a good time for these activities. You can use any pourable items, such as rice, split peas, lentils, sand, etc., instead of water in these activities.

Again, ask the children to estimate and get them to think about what they are doing.

Time

Time is an important factor in daily life but it is a difficult concept for young children to grasp. Digital watches are often given to children because they are modern, and because they are thought to make telling the time easier. I tell children that 'digital watches are for people who can't tell the time'. When a child tells me that it is 11.38 I usually ask, 'What does that mean?' Many children are unable to answer because they know nothing about minutes in an hour and so on. Children need to learn to tell the time; once they understand this they can use a digital watch. After all, digital watches are a great help in learning the 24-hour clock, which is something many junior school children find difficult.

Pre-school children will start by learning the hour, and may have learned the half-hour, quarter to and quarter past by the time they start full-time education. Most children, however, have little real understanding of time until they are six or seven.

The time of television programmes often helps with learning to tell the time, because if you can tell the time you won't miss your favourite programme!

MONEY

Shopping and pocket money bring in experiences of money and change. Talk about money and the different values of the coins, and let the children handle real money rather than plastic coins.

Most pre-school children are able to count accurately up to five, many up to ten, and some even further. Activities with money are limited by counting ability, but even so you can help them to see that five 1p coins equal a 5p coin and so on. Most pre-school children, and young infant school children, find the giving of change difficult to grasp. If you do not have the correct amount of pocket money, and change has to be given, always count it out as they do in shops.

EXTENDING VOCABULARY

All these activities give opportunities for extending the children's vocabularies. They could learn:

- the numbers up to five, and perhaps up to ten or even further;
- the colours;
- simple shapes, e.g. circle, triangle, square, rectangle;
- the coins;
- the hour, and possibly the half-hour and the quarters;
- the days of the week;
- words such as today, tomorrow and yesterday;
- the months of the year;
- the sequence of the seasons;
- words to do with counting – more than, less than, the same as, equals;
- words to do with measuring – bigger, smaller, taller, shorter, heavier, lighter, wider, narrower, thinner;
- how to use words such as beginning, end, near, far, inside, outside, over, under, top, bottom, front, back.

Number activities, as you can see, play an important part in our daily lives, and the experiences you give your child will create a valuable foundation for school later on. However, keep these

58 *Ready for School*

activities where they belong: as real activities in your everyday life. Don't turn them into meaningless sums on paper! All that you do at home should be done verbally and with objects that the children can handle. The only exception I suggest to this is that you teach your children to know how to form the number symbols 1–10 correctly. The traffic light system used for handwriting can be useful with this, too. Remember the importance of estimation in all mathematics, and the importance of enjoyment. Don't rush things or try to go too far too soon. Then the experience will be enjoyable for all of you.

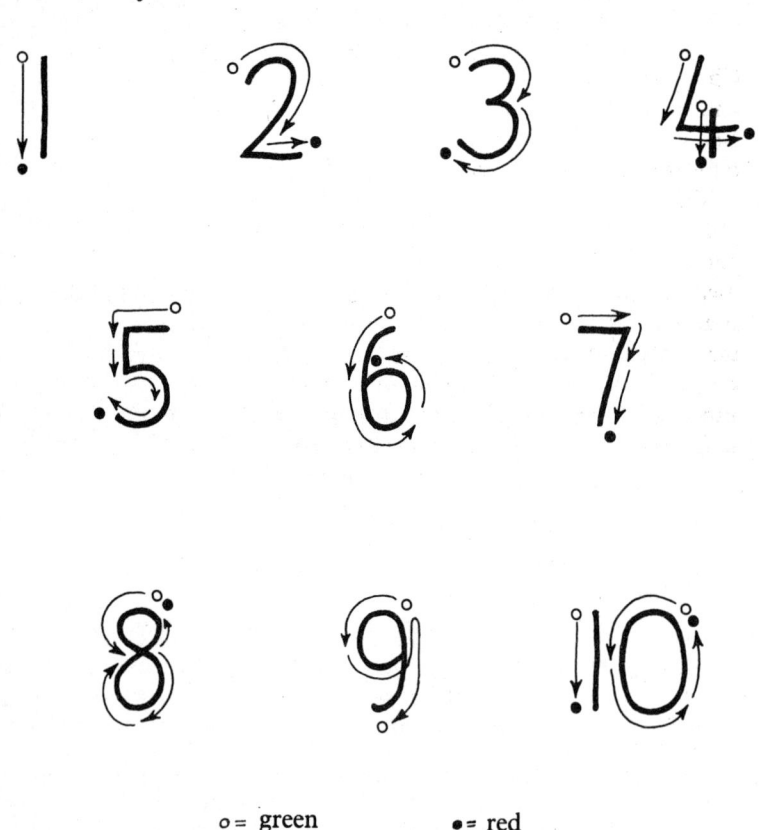

o = green   • = red

Chapters 2, 3 and 4 have been concerned with reading, writing and arithmetic, but education is far more than the basic three Rs. These *are* important, but education needs to be balanced if children are to grow up to be 'rounded' personalities.

Therefore, even in the pre-school years, you need to give children experiences that will awaken in them interest in science, their environment in general, art and craft, music, body awareness, the ability to socialize and the gradual growth of independence. This may sound a forbidding task, but it really isn't. Most of it is common sense, and I'm sure that as you read on you'll be able to say, 'Well I do that anyway.' Perhaps you see now what I meant at the beginning when I said that parents are educators, just as much as teachers are.

5
Kitchen science

What does the word science conjure up in your mind? Perhaps it creates a picture of laboratories with people in white coats peering into microscopes and carrying out complicated experiments. Science, however, like maths, is all around us in our everyday lives just waiting to be discovered. Scientists are keen to find out more about their specific areas of research. Your children are naturally curious, and with your help they can develop a greater understanding of their surroundings. The following sections will give you ideas on how to extend their scientific thinking.

PLAYING WITH WATER

Most children enjoy playing with water, in the sink, in the bath or outside in the summer. Babies enjoy bathtime, and relax in the warm water. Later, children enjoy experimenting with water and gradually they gain more control in handling it, as well as finding out more about its properties.

Water can make a mess so take precautions to protect clothing, floors and furniture. If it is a warm day, the children can play outside without clothes, and this makes everything much easier. When they play with water indoors, plastic aprons are useful for keeping most of them dry, and their sleeves should be securely rolled up. You can get elasticated armlets or cuffs to cover sleeves. A tiled or lino-covered floor is easy to mop up, but if you have a different surface cover it with a waterproof sheet, an old bath towel or a candlewick bedspread.

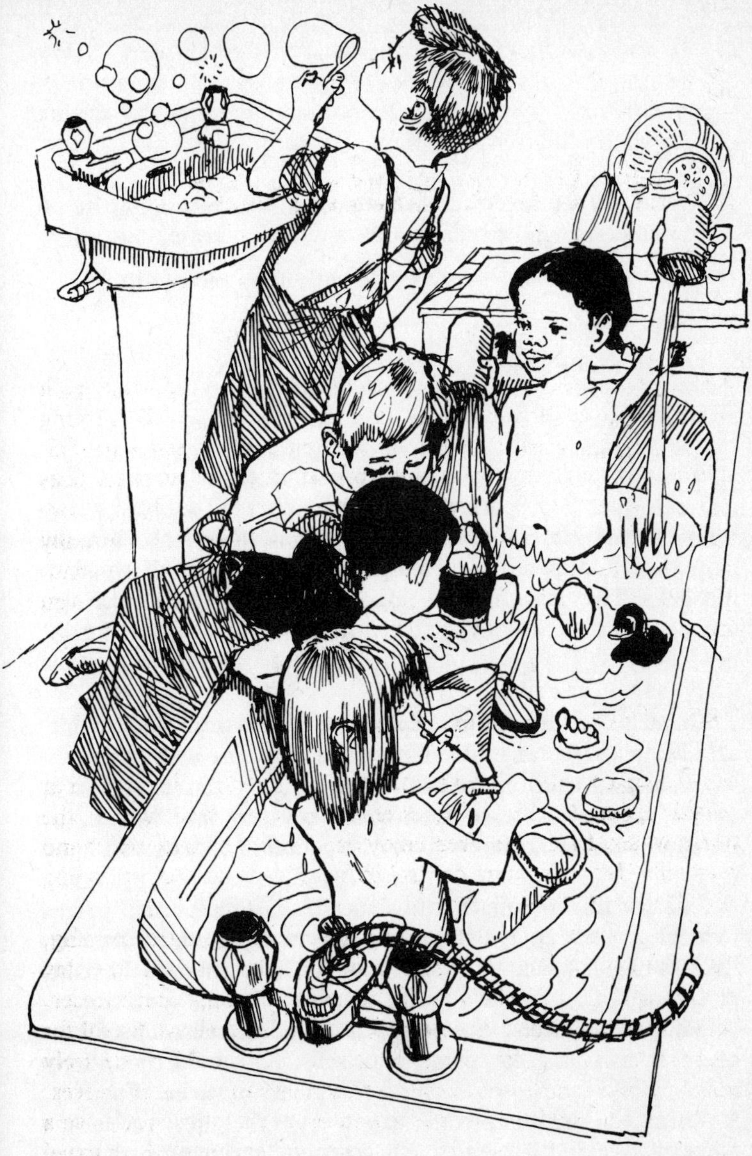

The water itself will give much pleasure, but if you make sure that a variety of other equipment is handy then the children's play can be extended. It is a good idea to use transparent containers so that children can see the water level, but glass containers are not safe for young children. Use plastic. Water play toys can include:

a variety of containers, e.g. shampoo bottles, washing-up liquid containers, yoghurt tubs, margarine tubs, jugs, tea-pot, cups;

sieve, colander, or plastic bottle with holes pierced in it;

plastic tubing;

funnels of different sizes;

corks, pieces of wood.

Water play gives you many opportunities for science. The children will enjoy floating a toy ship or duck on the bath water, but what other things will float, and which things sink? You can help the children make boats from corks, pieces of wood or nutshells. They can enjoy putting small items in them to see how much cargo they can carry. You could take this further and make boats out of foil, paper or plasticine. Again see how much they can carry before they sink.

Colouring water with food colouring adds variety, and bubbles are always a great favourite. You can add washing-up liquid to the water, and the children can enjoy blowing into it through straws or plastic tubes to increase the froth. They can have washing-up liquid in a cup and blow bubbles with a piece of wire twisted into a loop.

Children like to imitate adults and this is an important part of their play. They enjoy helping with the washing-up, hanging out the washing or washing the car. They can help you bath the baby, or can bath a doll while you dry their baby brother or sister.

While the children are playing with the water, relax and let them enjoy themselves. Allow plenty of time for this activity, but do stay near. A child can drown in only a few inches of water. When you stay near, the children can talk to you about their discoveries, and you can share in their enjoyment, knowing at the same time that they are safe.

PLAYING WITH SAND

Sand is another natural material that will give children hours of pleasure. Washed silver sand is the best for children, and will not stain like red builders' sand. If you have a garden you can make a sand pit, and the sand will be cleaned by the rain and the sun. It is, however, a good idea to make a cover so that dogs and cats are unable to foul it. If you live in a flat and don't have access to a garden, you can keep sand in a baby bath indoors. This will need to be cleaned from time to time by rinsing with disinfected water.

Wet and dry sand have very different properties so let the children explore and experiment with both. They will enjoy letting dry sand trickle through their fingers, sieving it and pouring it. When water is added the sand changes into a building material, and they will be able to use it for sand pies, castles and model villages. If you make sure that there are some of the following items near the sand, then the children's play can be extended:

various containers;
small spade, spoons, scoops;
sieve, colander;
plastic tubing;
bucket;
various moulds or cutters;
a small rake;
cars;
trucks, lorries, wheelbarrow for transporting the sand.

Make sure the children understand that they should not throw sand because it can damage eyes. If any sand does get into a child's eyes, wash them with plenty of cold water, or bathe them with wet cotton wool. Young children will often taste sand, and this won't hurt them, but if eaten it can cause diarrhoea, so it is best to discourage tasting sand.

COOKING

Cooking is an everyday occurrence that gives opportunities for the development of scientific thinking. Why does a mixture look different when it is cooked? What makes cakes and bread rise? Butter looks more or less the same when it has been heated up then cooled, so why don't meats or eggs? Where does the sugar go when you stir your tea or coffee? Why does butter or margarine melt when it is put on toast? Don't worry if you are unsure about the answers to these questions, and never be afraid to admit to the children that you don't know. Nobody is infallible and knows it all! It is much better to say to children that you don't know something and then suggest that you can find out the answer together.

Children often like to help with the cooking, and it is fun to eat something that you have cooked together. If the children want to make cakes or other items for their toy people they can use flour and salt dough. Once this has been baked they can paint and varnish it. Then they will have something that not only looks real but will last. Here are four recipes for play dough that you can try, or you can buy the commercially made Play Doh.

Recipes for play dough

1. The simplest play dough is made with three cups of self-raising flour to which water is added. It is not cooked. Food colour or powder paint can be added for variety. This makes a spongy, stretchy dough that will not keep, but it is so easy to make the children will enjoy making it themselves. It is a poking, rolling, pressing, squeezing type of dough. It will not model well but is pleasant just to handle.

2. A second recipe calls for two cups of plain flour, one cup of salt, water for mixing and colouring if desired. No cooking is required. Because of the salt content this dough has better keeping qualities, and if stored in a polythene bag or plastic box with a lid in a fridge it will be usable for a week or two. The plain flour in this recipe gives the dough a modelling quality, not unlike an odourless plasticine. Shapes made will retain their form, it handles well and is pleasant to use. If the children make this recipe and inadvertently add a large quantity of water, mix well and use as a finger paint.

3. As a third variation, mix three cups of plain flour, one cup of salt, one tablespoon of cooking oil and water as required. Add colouring if desired. Knead until well mixed and glossy. No cooking is required. This is a smooth, tough dough with a nice gleam. It is easily cut with pastry cutters, holds its shape when used for modelling and is pliable and pleasant to handle.

4. For a play dough with a different texture, try three cups of self-raising flour, add three cups of salt, colouring if desired and water until well mixed. This is a non-sticky dough which, because of the high salt content, feels gritty to the touch. The uncooked dough will be usable for up to a month if carefully stored, as the salt acts as a preservative. If left uncoloured, this dough can be baked hard in a slow oven and painted when cold. To save on fuel, pop a tray of modelled forms in the oven as it is slowly cooling after cooking a meal.

All the doughs are easy to remove from carpets. If they are left to dry out they will crumble and can easily be vacuumed away.

MAGNETS

If you have a magnet, children can have fun finding out what objects it will attract, what materials the magnetism will pass through and over what distance the magnetism will still attract. If you have more than one magnet, or a variety of types of magnet, so much the better. The children will be intrigued to find out that sometimes magnets attract, while in other situations they repel. Can they work out why, at least in their terms? You are not expected to teach your young children sixth form physics, so please keep it very simple. Even so, it is important that you take every chance to extend the children's language, while keeping everything at their level. This will mean that their learning will go hand-in-hand with understanding, and that their interest in learning won't wane.

LEARNING TO OBSERVE

The home, the local area and further afield all give valuable opportunities for environmental science. Children are fascinated by the changing seasons, the weather, growing plants, animals and other living things. They are curious about their surroundings and you can do much to help them to learn to observe in detail.

When you go out in the garden or for a walk, or wherever you are, point out things of interest, stop to look in hedges or on the underside of leaves. Do you know the names of trees and wild flowers that you pass? If not, try to identify them in library books or books you have at home. Collect frog spawn or toad spawn in the spring and watch the development cycle. Once the frogs or toads have developed, they should be returned to their natural habitat. Get the children to try to draw or paint the tadpoles, leaves, trees and insects they observe. Do their pictures really show the object being observed? Have they really used their eyes, or have they drawn what they thought might be there? Help them by pointing out the main details, and talking with them about their pictures – accurate observation won't happen overnight, it needs much practice.

If you live in a town, use the local park, building sites or wasteland in the same way. Building sites and wasteland can, however, be dangerous places, so take care.

THE WEATHER

The weather is a constant source of conversation, and changes in the weather give you plenty of activities to do with the children. Here are some suggestions for you to try:

On a windy day
Why do some clothes dry quicker than others?
Try to make a kite. Will it fly?

On rainy days
Collect rain and measure how much has fallen.
What sort of material is used to make waterproof clothes?

In snowy and frosty weather
Bring in a yoghurt carton of snow. How long does it take to thaw? Is the level of the water as high as the snow was?
Put out a yoghurt carton of water overnight. What happens when the water freezes? How long does it take to thaw when you bring it inside?

You could extend this activity even further by weighing the carton of snow then, when it has thawed, weighing the carton of water, and weighing it again when it has frozen. Don't forget to allow for the weight of the carton if you want to be accurate. On sunny days you could see how long it takes for the sun to evaporate a saucer of water on a window ledge, or for wet sand to dry; and you could time the clothes drying on the line. Do some dry more quickly than others and can you work out why?

GROWING THINGS

If you have a garden, an allotment, a window box, some house plants or even none of these, children will still be interested in planting and growing things. If they can have a small part of the garden or allotment to themselves, so much the better, but if this is not possible they can plant cress or a few seeds in a seed box to enjoy watching them grow. They can also experiment with growing carrot tops in a saucer of water, or grapefruit, orange, lemon or apple pips in polythene bags of damp compost hung up by a window – their own mini-greenhouse!

Bulbs are also fun to grow, and it causes great excitement when the first green shoot shows and they can be taken out of the dark hiding place. Bulbs also cheer up the house during the winter. You could extend the children's learning even further by growing seeds under different conditions – in the dark, without water, in the fridge, without compost – and letting the children find out what happens.

PETS

Many children like animals, and if they can have a pet they can learn how to look after it, and to take some responsibility for its welfare. Don't forget, however, that kittens grow into cats, and small puppies can grow into enormous dogs, taking up a good deal of space and being expensive to feed. Choose your pet according to the size of your house or flat, whether you live in a town or in the country, how much time you are prepared to spend on looking after it, and how much you can afford to spend on it week after week. Some pets, such as goldfish, canaries and budgies, take very little looking after and the children become just as attached to these as to larger, more expensive and more demanding pets. They will also enjoy watching birds. If you have a bird table or nesting box this will add to the fun. Here is a receipe for bird cake. The birds love this, and you can enjoy watching them while they eat.

Recipe for bird cake

You need breadcrumbs, currants, cooked potato, oatmeal and fat.

Method: Fill two yoghurt pots with a mixture of breadcrumbs, currants, cooked potato and oatmeal. Melt the fat, and pour one yoghurt pot of fat over the dry ingredients. Put the 'cake' in the fridge to cool and harden. Then hang it up on the bird table or from a tree.

VOCABULARY

Many of the activities and experiences included under the umbrella term of 'science', environmental or otherwise, will be verbal. You talk through the experiences with the children, and together try to work out what is happening in a way that makes sense to both of you. Consequently, you will have many opportunities to develop the children's 'scientific' language, as well as to extend their ability to observe what is really going on in the world around them. You could keep a chart to show which birds come into your garden or keep a diary of all the things you have grown, collected or seen. In this way you will have a record of all your observations.

6
Toys

CHOOSING TOYS

There are so many different toys on sale that it can be difficult to choose which ones to buy. Before you make your decision, ask yourself what use this particular toy will be to your children, how long it might last when in daily use and whether or not you think it is safe. It is also a good idea to stop and think whether or not you could make something at home that would do the same thing, but more cheaply.

Babies enjoy toys that make a noise, such as soft balls with a bell inside or a variety of rattles, and they like to watch mobiles when they are in the cot or the pram. Babies will explore their toys with their fingers, toes and mouths, so the toys need to be washable. They will enjoy banging them on the floor, the table or the side of the pram, as well as dropping them and inviting you to pick them up. A baby never seems to tire of this game, even though you will!

Toddlers like to play with cuddly toys, stacking toys, hammering toys, post boxes, construction toys and vehicles you can move about, in or on.

Young children of three and four enjoy more complicated construction toys, jigsaw puzzles, threading and sewing toys, simple games, playing with balls, dolls and other soft toys.

TOYS FROM JUNK

You could spend a fortune on toys, but really there is no need. Sometimes you will even find that a toy you have bought turns out to be a waste of money as it is hardly used. When our children were small we soon learned that we needn't really bother to buy toys, because the children always seemed more interested in playing with the wrappings rather than the gift. One Christmas our youngest child, who was then thirteen months old, spent the whole day climbing in and out of boxes, scrunching up wrapping paper and bedecking herself in coloured ribbon. What fun she had, and cheaply too!

What we see as rubbish or junk can give children much enjoyment and lead to valuable creative play. Many goods are packaged in boxes of various shapes and sizes. Waste products, such as tea packets, corn flake packets, egg boxes, chocolate boxes and cheese spread boxes, can be put to imaginative use by children, and they have certain advantages over bought toys. They cost nothing, are easily replaced, can be turned into a variety of things, and no one will be cross if you decide to squash them, sit on them or tear them up. A young child will happily sit putting items into a box and then emptying it or shaking it to make a noise. A four-year-old will be more imaginative and, if the box is big enough, will enjoy getting inside it and pretending it is a house, ship, aeroplane, spaceship or car. It can be fun to paint the box to make it more realistic. When the child loses interest in it, it can be demolished ready for the dustman to cart away.

BRICKS

Some toys remain popular with children over the years, and bricks are one of these. Babies will enjoy gripping a brick and exploring it with both hands and toes, as well as putting it in their mouths. They like the noise it makes when they bang it on the floor or on a saucepan. They will also enjoy knocking down a tower of bricks if you build one.

Toddlers will try to build a tower for themselves. At first they will only manage two or three bricks, but gradually they will be better balanced. They will then enjoy knocking the tower down and starting again.

Ready for School

By the time they are four, children will be creating buildings, castles and whole villages with bricks. They will be able to build co-operatively with their friends and will add cars, trees and play people to their constructions.

You can buy plastic bricks, and these are light to pick up and fairly cheap. After a while they tend to lose their shape or crack, so you may prefer to buy wooden bricks. These will be more expensive but they will last. They usually come in a duffle bag or trolley for easy storage. Buy as many bricks as you can afford, because it is very frustrating to run out of bricks before a building is completed.

DRESSING UP

Children love to dress up, and if you provide a box of dressing-up clothes you will add another dimension to their imaginative play. Old curtains, pieces of net, lace, ribbons, handbags and hats are more versatile than nurses' uniforms or cowboy suits, which can only be one thing. An old curtain, for example, can become a cloak, robe, bed cover, carpet, ghost, bride's train or sari.

PACKING AWAY

Encourage children to help tidy away their toys but to avoid too much disappointment give an advance warning before packing away begins. Even very young children can help with this activity, and it can become a game in itself.

7
Art and craft

MATERIALS

Children have a natural urge to draw, paint and make things. To keep them happy, your little ones will need supplies of paper, pencils, crayons, felt tips, paints, glue, scissors, cardboard and a wide variety of waste materials. Try to keep a stock in readiness, and store it in a large grocery box (covered with wallpaper to make it more attractive) or in a plastic laundry basket. Almost anything can be used by the children to make models, as long as it is not dangerous like glass. An interesting box of waste 'goodies' would include

boxes of all shapes and sizes, egg boxes, card and plastic egg trays, yogurt and cream cartons;
toilet-roll tubes and those from foil, cling film, etc.;
pipe cleaners;
pieces of string and balls of wall;
washed milk bottle tops;
sweet wrappers;
a variety of packaging, e.g. from chocolate boxes or biscuit tins;
cake cases;
polystyrene chippings or blocks;
cotton reels;
match-boxes;
scrap pieces of material;
washing-up liquid containers;
catalogues for cutting up.

Art and craft 75

You need to provide a good strong glue when the children are making models, because there is nothing more frustrating than to spend time creating a model only to watch it fall apart. Marvin medium is as good as anything, but buy the washable one, as the other kind quickly ruins clothes. Encourage children to roll up their sleeves and put on something protective when they are going to do a 'messy' activity. Aprons really only protect the children's fronts, although there are some waterproof ones with sleeves. Better still, and cheaper too, use an old shirt, which can be washed when necessary.

Children need to develop gradually what educationists call 'fine motor skills', which include pencil and paint-brush control and scissor dexterity. The art activities mentioned in this chapter all help with this.

PAINTING

Young children tend to get paint over everything within reach, so protect floors and furniture. Newspaper or a polythene sheet will keep paint off most surfaces. You can buy unbreakable non-spill paint pots, or make your own by cutting down washing-up liquid bottles.

Good painting paper is expensive, but newspaper, the back of used computer paper, wallpaper, posters and wrapping paper are all cheap to provide. Remember to provide large pieces of paper – the younger the child the larger the piece of paper needed. You can vary the painting activity by:

1. Providing different shaped pieces of paper – circles, triangles, hexagons, thin strips or irregular shapes.
2. Finger painting – with extra thick paint, using fingers rather than a brush.
3. Sponge painting – provide a small sponge or piece of foam rubber instead of a brush
4. Printing patterns – using cotton reels, halved potatoes, leaves, etc.

5. Splatter painting – blow paint on to the paper with a straw. This can be very messy!
6. Paint on half the paper, then fold over onto the other half to make a symmetrical pattern.
7. Add items to a finished painting – wool for hair, laces on shoes, etc.

I have mentioned that children like to imitate adults, so if you are painting the house let the children have a washed-out paint tin filled with water, and they can 'paint' the bricks at the same time.

Painting is an absorbing activity for young children, and it can give a welcome release for pent-up feelings of anger, fear or sadness. The children may want to talk about their paintings and to share them with you, but at other times they may prefer to work in silence. Don't be surprised at this; children as well as adults need privacy.

ART WORK FROM THE SEASONS

The seasons also give opportunities for a variety of art work:

Autumn
collecting and pressing leaves for pictures;
leaf prints;
collage pictures using leaves.

Winter
snowflake designs;
snowman mobiles;
Christmas cards;
Christmas calendars.

Spring
seed pictures;
'observed' drawings of bulbs as they flower.

Summer
collecting and pressing flowers for pictures;
pressed flower cards;
bark rubbings.

MODELLING

Modelling with plasticine could lead on to modelling with flour and salt dough or with clay. Whenever I used plasticine the brightly coloured sticks quickly ended up greenish-grey. I had more success with play dough, and this works out very cheaply when you make your own. You will find several recipes in the section on cooking in the previous chapter.

The most satisfying medium, however, is clay and the children enjoy the feel of it in their hands. You could show the children how to make simple 'thumb' pots, tiles or basic models. You probably won't be able to fire the pots, but if you allow them to dry out slowly they can then be varnished. There is also available a special clay that gives good results without being fired.

OTHER ART AND CRAFT ACTIVITIES

1. Scrap books can provide hours of useful and enjoyable activity, especially when the weather is bad or the children are 'off colour'. They cost very little yet give plenty of practice in cutting, sticking and arranging.
2. Coloured gummed paper can be used to make pictures and patterns.
3. Painting books, colouring books, dot-to-dot books, magic painting books and puzzle pages in comics all help to develop and improve the children's dexterity.
4. Simple sewing, lacing and threading toys.
5. Models from waste materials, which can then be painted.

These are only a few of the art and craft activities the children would enjoy. I'm sure that you can think of many more. Again, however, I want to stress the importance of talking about what you and the children are doing while you are doing it, so extending the children's vocabulary wherever possible.

8
Music at home

We must look forward to the time when all people in all lands are brought together through singing, and when there is a universal harmony.

Zoltán Kodály, 1937

Earlier in this book I said that there is music in every child but that it needs to be brought out. Let me explain what I mean.

Babies quickly learn to recognize their mother's voice and to react to a wide variety of sounds, such as loud and soft sounds, angry voices and calming reassuring voices. Music is sound and from birth children react to the stimulus of music. When your baby is on your lap or in the bath, you probably sing or say the well-known nursery rhymes or rhymes such as:

Round and round the garden,
Like a teddy bear.
One step, two step (walk up the arm with your fingers),
Tickle up there (under the arm);

Ten little fingers, ten little toes,
Two little eyes, and one little nose.

As you say these rhymes you touch the baby's fingers, toes and face to help build up body awareness. You say the rhymes with the baby close to you and this body contact will help in tightening the bond between you.

Your baby will want you to repeat these rhymes over and over again, and the sound of them will become very familiar. Gradually the baby will begin to do some of the actions and to say a few words of each rhyme.

NURSERY RHYMES

Hearing and learning a wide variety of nursery rhymes will create an early enjoyment of music. When people are happy they often show this by singing or whistling. If you show your child that you enjoy singing he or she will want to join in with you. A child will need to hear the same song many times before the patterns of sound will be remembered, so sing over and over again the favourite rhymes, such as: Baa, Baa Black Sheep', 'Humpty-Dumpty', 'Sing a Song of Sixpence', 'Twinkle, Twinkle Little Star', and 'Pop Goes the Weasel'.

Singing these rhymes and others in the bath, at bedtime or on a journey gives much pleasure, but it also introduces the children to patterns of notes and the variety of musical intervals that they can hear and sing.

RHYTHM AND MOVEMENT

Babies enjoy movement and find it soothing. They will often go to sleep if you rock them on your shoulder or in your arms, or if you push them in the pram. They will also enjoy being 'bumped' on your knee while you sing 'Ride a Cock Horse', or playing 'See-Saw' while you see 'See-saw Marjory Dawe'. Later, when they are about two and a half to three years old, they will get much enjoyment from circle games, such as 'Ring-a-Ring-a-Roses' and 'The Farmer's in His Den'. They will continue to enjoy these games when they go to play group and even after they go to infant school.

Circle games encourage children to listen to the rhythm of the words and to move in time with them. Words have a natural rhythm and learning to respond to the music of words will help young children with reading and writing later on. (This point was mentioned in Chapter 2, p. 15.)

SOUNDS

Sounds make up words, and sounds also form music. Around your house there are many sounds that you can listen to with your child, and the sounds each have their own rhythm. Take a 'listening' walk around the house and see how many different sounds you can hear. Imitate the sounds, such as the tick-tock of the clock or the whine of the washing machine as it spins.

Young children enjoy making their own sounds by banging spoons on a table or crashing saucepan lids. You can help them to realize that sounds can be loud or soft, fast or slow, and can vary in speed and volume of sound, by 'playing' examples for them to repeat back to you. Home-made shakers and drums, as mentioned in Chapter 2, could be used for this. Children also enjoy experimenting on a small xylophone.

Music, therefore, starts in the cradle, and can continue to give pleasure throughout life. Music is fun, so enjoy it and join in with the children's musical activities.

9
Body awareness

What does body awareness mean? Children are aware that they have bodies, but they will need your help in finding out all the activities of which their bodies are capable.

ACTIVITIES FOR TODDLERS

Toddlers are not very well co-ordinated and they need practice to improve their ability to walk, then run. Some of them, of course, want to run before they can walk. Once the children can walk you can introduce walking sideways, or backwards (as long as you remind them to look over a shoulder), round and round, or a combination of all of these. This activity brings in directional language, including counting and the meaning of left and right. 'Can you walk five steps forwards, four backwards, three to the left, then three to the right?' What a lot to concentrate on! If you have paving slabs outside or carpet or lino tiles inside, these can become part of this game.

ACTIVITIES FOR FOUR- AND FIVE-YEAR-OLDS

Later, when the children are steadier on their feet and gaining more confidence, encourage them to jump, hop and skip. This can lead on to hopscotch – again your slabs or tiles will prove useful – and to combination movements such as a hop, a skip and a jump.

Encourage the children to experiment and to see, for example, how many different kinds of jump they can think of. Can they perform these in a sequence?

ACTIVITIES TO INCREASE CO-ORDINATION

Foot, hand and eye co-ordination are important for everyone. Body awareness activities that come first to mind include ball control and throwing and catching. Little children need to use a large ball (a foam one is often best). Encourage the children to keep their eye on the ball, to get their body behind it, to catch it with both hands and to cradle it against their tummy. These instructions probably sound very obvious but some children go to school never having played with a ball. Play ball games with your three- and four-year-olds and when they can throw and catch fairly well, extend the ways in which they can control the ball: bouncing with the feet, hitting with a bat and controlling with a variety of parts of the body – head, knees, fist, etc. Later, when their control is much improved, make the activities more difficult by, for example, throwing and catching over a wider distance, decreasing the size of the ball, changing the type of ball and asking them to negotiate cones while bouncing or dribbling the ball. These activities may, however, have to wait until they are five or six.

SWIMMING

Swimming is a marvellous sport for people of all ages, and is something you can enjoy with the children. Many public pools have 'water babies' sessions, when parents can swim with their young children and even babies. If your local pool offers this facility, make the most of it and start your children as early as possible.

BODY SHAPES

Earlier (p. 27) I mentioned drawing large letter shapes, based on whole body movements, for children interested in writing. This is a very useful activity for reinforcing correct formation and could lead on to the children experimenting to see what other types of shape they can make with their bodies; thin shapes, wide shapes, low shapes, high shapes, spiky shapes, threatening shapes, round shapes and so on.

This is not only fun to do (and you can join in too), it also gets the children concentrating, using their imagination and developing their language. Music adds another dimension and leads the children into dance. Exercises done to music are fun, and they are even more meaningful if you combine them with instructions such as:

> Touch your left foot with your right hand.
> Put your head on your left knee.
> Make a circle movement with your right foot.
> Lie on the floor, put both legs in the air and try to touch the floor behind your head. (You may find this harder than the children!)

The activity is fun, but it also includes listening to instructions, carrying them out, practising 'left' and 'right' and increasing body awareness.

Body awareness activities are important for the children and will keep you fit, too!

10
Getting on with others

Babies are utterly dependent upon you for food, comfort, shelter and love. They gradually learn to do more for themselves. They will learn to feed themselves and later dress themselves, but they still need you near to give security. Some babies will happily allow others to cuddle them and feed them, but others make it obvious that they prefer mother or father.

Toddlers gradually become more outward looking and enjoy the company of others of their own age. If you are lucky enough to live where there are plenty of other children the same age as yours, it is easy to arrange for them to play together. If you live in a more isolated area or there are no other young children in your vicinity, it will be more difficult for you to provide opportunities for your children to play with others. Even if it means quite a lot of travelling, it really will be worth the effort.

COPING WITH PARTINGS: JOINING THE GROUP

Young children are very self-centred and find it difficult to consider anyone other than themselves. It can be a hard lesson learning to share, to take turns, to become part of a group and to cope with being away from parents for short periods of time. If other children come to play, your children will have to learn to share you with the others. When your children go to play at a friend's house, they have to learn to relate to another adult, to realize that there may be different 'house rules' in another house and to accept that you will return to collect them. Learning to cope with being separated from you and learning to become part of a group are difficult lessons for many young children. Playing with friends, going to a mother and toddler group and going to a play group will all help children with these social activities. Even so, when they start full-time schooling, many children will still be learning to cope with being parted from you and the family group. This is quite natural. Although the child's tears can be upsetting, they rarely last long after the parent has disappeared. If your child is really upset the teacher will invite you to stay for a while.

SHARING

For many children, sharing is another difficult lesson to learn. 'Why should I?' or 'But it's mine' will have been heard by many parents, but it would be an unpleasant world if everyone said this! Yes, some toys *may* be broken or spoiled by visitors, or by your own children. Perhaps a very special toy could be put away if a particularly boisterous child is coming to play. On the whole most toys do survive.

Taking turns often has to be learned in conversation as well as in games. When children want to speak they often just do so, even if someone else is already speaking. It is difficult to learn to wait and listen to another, when what you want to say is very important and in your opinion so much more interesting! But if children are to relate to others this is a lesson they must learn, even if it does mean that sometimes they have forgotten what they want to say by the time they can say it.

Games bring many other opportunities for sharing and taking turns. When playing with others the children should be encouraged to take turns at choosing what they are going to do. Circle games give opportunities for taking turns because all the children can't be in the middle at once, or there would be no circle. Toddlers may find it very difficult to let another have a go with their stacking toy or posting game, while slightly older ones will have to learn to share their tricycle, construction kit or model. Later, when they play with card and board games, children have to take turns, and will need to get to grips with winning and losing. This is another hard lesson for children, and indeed is something that some adults continue to find difficult. The world, however, is full of all kinds of competition and so children need to experience this.

If you make sure that your children play regularly with others of a similar age and gain experience of being away from you for short intervals, they will learn to become less self-centred and a little more concerned for others. Alongside this is the development of independence, the subject of the next chapter.

11
Growing independence

When you have a family you undertake to look after the children, to take responsibility for them and to educate them. At the same time, however, you realize that if you are to do this job well, you must aim to lead the children from utter dependence upon you to absolute independence from you. If you are unable to 'cut the apron strings' you have not completed your task.

The children from birth to school age will have travelled only a short way along the road towards independence. Even so, you should guard against 'spoon-feeding' them. While they are babies you have to do everything for them but gradually as they grow they will want to do more and more for themselves and you should encourage them in this.

FEEDING

The first attempts babies make to feed themselves are usually very messy affairs. This is not disastrous as long as you take the necessary precautions – a good plastic bib with a 'drip tray', wipe-down surfaces and newspaper or a plastic sheet on the floor. Afterwards the children may need a mini bath, but what a feeling of success they will have. Success usually breeds success. Once one hurdle is overcome, others will be attempted until the child can cope competently enough to manage more or less alone.

DRESSING

Dressing can become a battle area! Once children are interested in dressing themselves they tend to take a long time over it and they can suddenly have very strong likes and dislikes about what they will or won't wear. Yes, it does take longer but it is worth it, unless you are going to miss the bus or train in the attempt. If there are no time constraints, you don't have to stay and watch the performance if you have other jobs to do. As long as the children are safe to be left in the room alone, it doesn't matter if items of clothing are on inside-out or back to front. Always give plenty of praise when the children have tried hard. Gradually the time span will decrease and the end product will be much more presentable!

TOILET TRAINING

Toilet training is another area in which the children need to have gained independence before they go to school. They will still have 'accidents', especially if they are particularly absorbed in an activity, if they are off-colour or if the weather is bitterly cold. This is to be expected, but for the most part they should be dry and clean. It would also be a great help at school if all children learned to flush the toilet after use and then to wash their hands. This is a plea often made by infant teachers.

ENCOURAGE YOUR CHILDREN TO HELP

Other jobs that young children should be encouraged to do are:

1. Picking up their toys and books and putting them away.
2. Setting and clearing tables, even if they only put out and clear away the mats and place the cutlery ready.
3. Folding clothes.
4. Helping to clear up after art and craft sessions.
5. They will also enjoy 'helping' you do the housework, shopping, gardening and other household jobs.

Find out what is on offer in your area regarding pre-school facilities, and make sure that, if at all possible, your children take part in some form of pre-school education. All the activities I have mentioned in this chapter will increase the children's independence, but children also need time away from you and the security that your presence gives, as explained in the previous chapter.

12
Starting school

When your children are about four years old it is time to decide which school you would like them to attend. Go and see all the schools in your area. Make up your mind after you have spoken with the head teacher and seen around each school in turn.

When the head teacher shows you around, do be ready to ask questions and don't be afraid to take a list with you so that you won't forget what it is that you want to find out. Your questions might include some of the following:

When will be child be able to start school?
How many children are there in a class?
What are the times of the school day?
Are the school meals cooked on the premises?
Do you use reading schemes? If so, which ones?
Do you use a maths scheme? If so, which one?
Is there a school uniform?
Do you let parents help in the school? If so, with what kinds of activities?
Is there a PTA (Parent Teacher Association)?
What extra-curricular activities are offered, e.g. football, netball, swimming, chess, folk-dancing, music?

While you are being shown around, bear in mind the following points:

Look at the displays – are they attractive and well displayed?
Does the school look cheerful and cared for?

Starting school

Does the head teacher know all the children by name, and how do the children react to the head teacher?
How do the staff react to the head teacher?
How do the non-teaching staff react to the head teacher?

In this way you will get a good idea of the character of the school. Then decide on the school where the atmosphere, philosophy and layout felt right for you and the children. Don't be tempted to make your decision on hearsay, local gossip or what you have read in the local paper. Make up your own mind based on what you have seen and the opinions you formed during your visits, bearing in mind what you feel is right for your children.

Once you have decided, be prepared to support the school and really get to know it. Near the beginning of the book I expressed the hope that parents and teachers would get together and that friction could be avoided. Once tension occurs between parents and the school, or among parents, then learning is impeded and children can suffer.

13
Summing up

Looking back over this book I hope that I have not made your task seem too daunting. My intention in writing was to show you the many ways in which you could build at home sound foundations for your children's education, ways that are fun, that need not be expensive and that really depend mainly upon your time, patience and common sense.

Anyone can be a good 'parent educator' if they are prepared to put in time and effort. If you have bothered to find the time to read this book, then I feel certain that you will make a good job of bringing up your children. Always remember that each child is an individual, and therefore unique, and so guard against comparisons within the family or with other people's children. Cherish your children, they are valuable and they are the country's future.

Book list

Here are some 'books about books' with suggestions for books that you can share with your children, including poetry. Ask your local librarian for suggestions and spend time in the library and in book shops, looking at children's books.

Bennett, Jill. *Learning to Read with Picture Books*. Thimble Press, Stroud.
Butler, Dorothy. *Cushla and Her Books*. Hodder & Stoughton, Sevenoaks.
Butler, Dorothy. *Babies Need Books*. Pelican, Harmondsworth. (Also useful for rhymes and fingerplays.)
Cutting, Brian. *Reading Matters*. Arnold Wheaton, Exeter.
Elkin, Judith (editor). *Books for Keeps. Guide to Children's Books for a Multicultural Society, 0–7*. Chequer Press,
Good Book Guide to Children's Books. Penguin, Harmondsworth.
Meek, Margaret. *Learning to Read*. Bodley Head, London.
Stories to Read and to Tell. YLG Pamphlet 21.
Trelease, Jim. *The Read Aloud Handbook*. Penguin, Harmondsworth.
Wisbey, Audrey. *Learn to Sing to Learn to Read*. BBC Publications, London.

The following organizations publish helpful book lists:
National Book League, 45 East Hill, London SW18 2QZ.
Signal Bookguides, Thimble Press, Station Road, South Woodchester, Stroud, Glos. GL5 5EQ.
Useful magazines are:

Books for Keeps   *Growing Point*
Books for Your Children *Signal Selection of Children's Books*
Good Book Guide

BOOKS FOR CHILDREN

Board books
Hill, Eric. *Little Spots*. Heinemann, London.
Jessel, Camilla. *Baby's Day* and *Baby's Toys*. Methuen, London.
Oxenbury, Helen. *Board Books*. Walker Books, London.
Pooh Board Books. Methuen, London.

Rhymes and fingerplays
Bennett, Jill (editor). *Roger Was a Razor Fish and Other Poems*. Hippo Books, London.
Briggs, Raymond. *The Mother Goose Treasury*. Puffin, Harmondsworth.
Ireson, Barbara (editor). *The Young Puffin Book of Verse*. Puffin, Harmondsworth.
Matterson, Elizabeth (editor). *This Little Puffin*. Puffin, Harmondsworth.
Milne, A.A. *When We Were Very Young*. Methuen, London.
Milne, A.A. *Now We Are Six*. Methuen, London.
Ormerod, Jan. *Rhymes around the Day*. Puffin, Harmondsworth.
Oxenbury, Helen. *Nursery Rhyme Book*. Heinemann, London.
Oxford Nursery Song Book. Oxford University Press, Oxford.
Play Group Association Booklet.
Voake, Charlotte (illustrator). *Over the Moon: a Book of Nursery Rhymes*. Walker Books, London.

Alphabet books
Crowther, Robert. *The Most Amazing Hide-and-Seek Alphabet Book*. Viking Kestrel, London.
Hughes, Shirley. *Lucy and Tom's a.b.c.* Puffin, Harmondsworth.
Wendon, Lyn. *Pictogram System*. Cambridge Aids to Learning, Cambridge. (Also available from: Pictogram Supplies, Barton, Cambridge CB3 7AY.)

Counting books
Bang, Molly. *Ten, Nine, Eight*. Puffin, Harmondsworth.
Bucknall, Caroline. *One Bear All Alone*. Macmillan, London.
de Brunhoff, Laurent. *Babar's Counting Book*. Methuen, London.

Index

Alphabet 27, 29, 30, 40
Anxiety 7, 8
Art 74–7

Bird cake (recipe) 69
Body awareness 81–3
Books
  alphabet 30
  list 93–4
  parts of 12–13
  pre-school years 19–20
  sharing 12, 20
  without text 13
Bricks 71–2

Capacity 56
Colouring 17, 21
Comics 16, 18
Cooking 54, 64
Counting 52–3, 57
Craft 74–7
Creative play 71–2

Dictionary 40
Drawing 17, 22
Dressing 88
Dressing-up 72

Estimation 53–6, 58

Finger play rhymes 13, 14, 93

Games
  card and board 86
  memory training 14
  jigsaw puzzles 16
  taking turns 85
Growing things 67

Imagination 12, 13, 15, 18, 19, 71, 72, 83
Independence 87–9
Instruments 15, 80

Junk 70–1

Left–right awareness 16, 17, 25, 34, 83
Letters
  capitals 21, 25, 30, 40
  formation 21, 26–9, 50
  lower case 21, 25, 30, 40
  names 30
  sounds 14, 30
  upper case 21, 25, 30, 40
Library 12, 15, 18, 66, 93
Listening 14, 15, 83

Magnets 65
Measuring 54
Memory 13, 14, 19, 25, 27, 48
Modelling 77
Money 57

Movement 15, 17, 27, 80–3
Music 15, 78–80

Numbers 50–8
  formation of 58
Nursery rhymes 13, 15, 78, 79

Observation 66, 69

Painting 22, 75, 76
Pencil grips 24
Pets 68, 69
Pictogram system 30–1
Play dough 64, 65, 77
Play groups 8, 15, 80, 85, 89
Prediction 13

Radio 15
Reading 10–20
Relationships 84–6, 91
Repetition 13, 19
Rhythms 15–17, 49, 80

Sand 27, 56, 63

School 8, 31, 85, 88, 90–1
Science 60–9
Scribble 21, 31
Sequencing 16, 17, 53
Shape 16, 25, 26
Sharing 85
Singing 13, 15, 18, 79
Sorting 50–2
Speech 10–12, 52, 57, 65, 69, 77, 85
Spelling 10, 40, 48–9
Swimming 82

Tapes 15, 19
Television 15, 56
Threading 17
Time 56
Toilet training 88
Toys 70–3

Water 56, 60–2
Weather 66
Weighing 54, 67
Wisbey, Dr Audrey 15
Writing 10, 21–49